Strange Bridges

Written by Isabel Thomas

Collins

Mind the gap!

Engineers make bridges to cross rivers, seas and valleys.

valley

This Japanese bridge is taller in the middle to let ships pass.

The road plunges like a rollercoaster!

3

Dragon Bridge

Bridges are pushed and pulled by traffic and wind, so engineers choose strong shapes like arches.

These arches have been turned into a dragon!
The head even makes fire!

Large bridge

Engineers made this bridge with arches and triangles. Triangles are very strong. It's hard to push or pull them out of shape.

The steel weighs as much as
500 blue whales.

Pulley bridge

Every time a tall ship comes along this river, gigantic **pulleys** raise the roadways!

pulleys

roadways

giant pylon

9

Tilting bridge

This bridge is for people and bikes.

When a boat needs to pass, the bridge tilts on giant hinges.

hinge

Glass bridge

Could you cross a bridge made from glass?
The glass lets people see the gorge below.

The bridge can carry the weight of eight hundred people at once.

gorge

Cracking bridge

Most bridges try to make people feel safe. This bridge teases people by pretending to crack!

The glass will not collapse.
It is safe. Phew!

Fun bridge

This bridge is a Ferris wheel too! If there is a traffic jam, people can look at the wheel going around.

Each pod carries
eight passengers.

Wildlife bridge

Not all bridges are for
people or cars. Every year,
crowds of crabs **migrate**
from land to sea.

This bridge helps crabs cross a road.

19

Your turn!

Could you be an engineer and invent a new kind of bridge?

Try to make your bridge strong and fun!

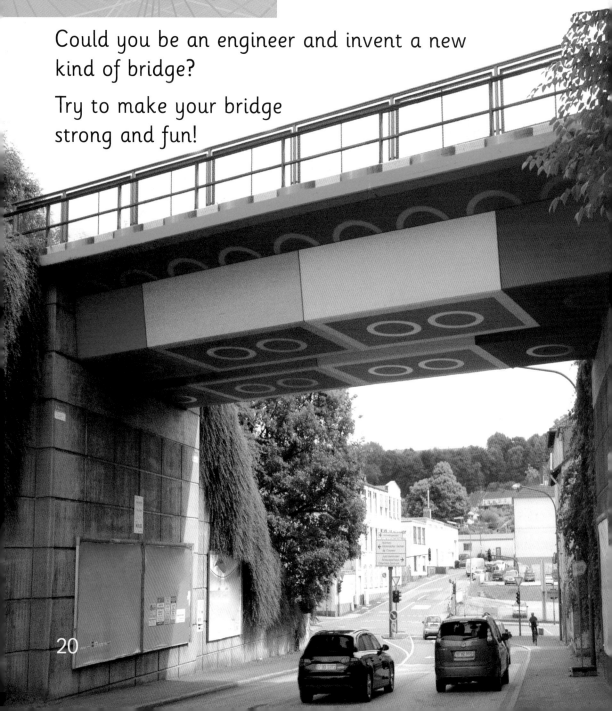

21

Bridges

After reading

Letters and Sounds: Phase 5

Word count: 294

Focus phonemes: /ai/ eigh /ee/ e-e, ey, e, y /oo/ u /igh/ y /c/ ch /j/ g, ge, dge /l/ le /f/ ph /w/ wh /v/ ve /s/ se /z/ se

Common exception words: into, to, the, of, are, people, once

Curriculum links: Geography: Human and physical geography; Design and technology: Technical knowledge

National Curriculum learning objectives: Reading/word reading: apply phonic knowledge and skills as the route to decode words; read accurately by blending sounds in unfamiliar words containing GPCs that have been taught; read other words of more than one syllable that contain taught GPCs; read aloud accurately books that are consistent with their developing phonic knowledge, re-read books to build up their fluency and confidence in word reading; Reading/comprehension: link what they have read or hear read to their own experiences; discuss word meanings; discuss the significance of the title and events

Developing fluency

- Your child may enjoy hearing you read the book.
- Reread your child's favourite page together.

Phonic practice

- Look through the book together.
- Ask your child:
  - Can you spot words with the /j/ sound written in different ways? (*strange, bridge, engineers, large, plunges, hinge, gorge*)
- In the book the author uses the word **phew**. How many words can you think of with the grapheme "ph" in? (e.g. *phew, photo, phone, dolphin, graph, elephant, nephew*)

Extending vocabulary

- Discuss what other words you could use in the title instead of the word **strange**. (e.g. *unusual, weird, odd, bizarre, different, extraordinary*)
- Look at the glossary on page 21. Ask your child:
  - What is a glossary? (e.g. *a glossary explains the meaning of technical vocabulary in the book*)
  - What does the word **engineers** mean? (e.g. *people who plan how to make something*)
  - Choose a word from the book. How would you describe it in the glossary? (e.g. *glimpse: to catch sight of*)